Space Explorers
MOON

First Published in Great Britain in 2020 by Buttercup Publishing Ltd.
46 Syon Lane, Isleworth, Greater London, TW7 5NQ, UK

Copyright © Buttercup Publishing Ltd. 2020
All rights reserved. No part of this book may be reproduced or transmitted in any form or by any electronic or mechanical means, including information storage and retrieval systems, without permission in writing from the publisher.

Author: Andrea Kaczmarek
Illustrator: Alexandra Colombo
Series Editor: Kirsty Taylor

A Cataloguing-in-Publishing record for this book is available from the British Library.

ISBN: 978-1-912422-92-0

www.buttercuppublishing.co.uk
contact@buttercuppublishing.co.uk
Printed and bound in China

Twins, Daisy and Dan, were back at Grandpa's house. They stood in the garden staring up at the big night sky.

"Where is the moon, Grandpa?" Dan said. "I can't see it! All I can see is a funny-looking banana surrounded by stars!"

"That's the moon, Dan. It changes shape." Grandpa pointed to the 'funny-looking banana' in the sky. "Sometimes it is round, like it was when we went on our last science adventure, and sometimes it looks like this."

"Can we get in our spaceship again and explore some more?" Dan pleaded.

The three of them scurried up the winding stairs to the very top of the house where the telescope sat. The twins were delighted to see their spaceship, COSMODAISYDAN again.

"Another space lesson before our explorers set off. You know the rules!"

"OK, Grandpa. Can I be the sun again?" Daisy asked, already reaching for the orange that sat in the room.

"Yes, and Dan, you can be the moon. Don't eat your banana this time!" Grandpa gave Dan a watchful glare. "I'll be Earth again."

Dan, as the moon, circled around Grandpa, as Earth.

Grandpa showed the twins a colourful poster that had funny words on it. "The Sun, or our Daisy, always shines bright." Daisy grinned a big grin, she almost glowed!

"Now remember, the Earth tilts and moves slowly around the Sun and the Moon moves around Earth." Grandpa pointed to the poster. "The Moon has no light of its own. The light you see shining from it is actually sunlight that is reflecting off it."

The twins gasped.

Grandpa continued to explain, "the part of the Moon facing the Sun is lit up, but the part of the Moon facing away from the Sun is in darkness. That's how it gets its shapes. We mainly see the part reflected by the Sun."

"I understand, Grandpa" Daisy said, as she sat down with a torch. "A half moon is very pretty, but my favourite is the full bright white moon." She shone the torch at the banana sitting on Dan's head.

"Me too, Daisy, but we won't see that kind of moon again until next week now. We better get our spaceship and telescope ready, science explorers!" Grandpa exclaimed.

Daisy and Dan loved learning about the moon, so they decided to make their own poster. They drew the shapes of the moon on a big sheet of paper, using white and yellow crayons.

"A full moon is big and round." Daisy scribbled neatly on the big sheet of paper in white and yellow. "And a half moon is exactly that. Half of the moon. That's all we can see!"

Moon

Earth

Daisy gave a yellow crayon to Dan. "A crescent moon is only small because there isn't much light on it from the sun. It's just a curve of the moon really – it looks a bit like your banana, Dan! You can't eat it though …" Daisy laughed.

Frowning, Dan scribbled his crescent moon onto the big sheet of paper, ignoring Daisy's moon-eating comment.

"I'm impressed, science explorers!" Grandpa said, smiling down at the twins. "I think we are ready to travel. Let's wait until next week when the full moon will appear."

Grandpa began to rummage through a wonky, red cupboard. "What are you doing, Grandpa?" Daisy asked.

"Well, we will need big boots and a helmet if we're going to the moon! It's very hard to walk in your slippers up there!"

"Why is it hard to walk on the moon, Grandpa?" puzzled Dan.

"Well, firstly, I don't want your feet to get cold in your slippers. Your Mum wouldn't thank me for that."

The children giggled and stared up at Grandpa quizzically. "The moon isn't like planet Earth. It has no air or clouds." Grandpa said.

"Or bananas!" Dan interrupted.

Grandpa raised his eyebrow and Daisy frowned. "No, Dan. No bananas. It has a lot of moon-dust instead. The most important thing that is missing, is gravity. If I drop my orange here on Earth, it will fall to the ground, but if I drop it on the moon, it will float."

Grandpa dropped the orange onto the floor.

The twins laughed, "So, the moon looks like a banana and has floating oranges?"

Grandpa rolled his eyes and smiled.

"The air is also dangerous up there, it's not like it is on Earth. We will need to make special boxes for our heads with tubes running to a box on our back. We can fill it with clean air."

Grandpa pulled out a funny-looking hat and backpack and gave one each to the twins. He was having fun getting the little science explorers ready.

"We have to walk slowly, too. Like this …" Grandpa moved his heavy foot carefully and so slowly that the twins laughed.

"You look funny, Grandpa!" Dan tried to copy, he almost toppled over!

The next week had arrived and the twins couldn't wait for their trip to the moon.
They wore their special hats and funny backpacks and practised their walk one more time.

After a little nap in COSMODAISYDAN - as all the best science explorers nap - Grandpa woke them gently. "No clouds tonight. The moon is big and bright. Let's have a look through the telescope. One at a time now!" The twins scrambled to the window. They couldn't wait to start their moon adventure.

What a sight it was. It was big, and round, and grey, but it had a beautiful silvery shine. They could see lots of funny-looking circles. They almost looked like holes! Grandpa told the twins that these are called craters. They saw mountains, too!

"Isn't she wonderful, our lovely Luna." Grandpa smiled at his little science explorers as they took turns looking through the big, red telescope.

"Who is Luna?" Daisy turned to Grandpa, with a confused look on her face.

"Some people call the moon, Luna. It is her other name," Grandpa explained. Daisy yawned, and Dan had already crawled back in to COSMODAISYDAN.

"I wish my name was Luna, too." Daisy could hardly keep her eyes open.

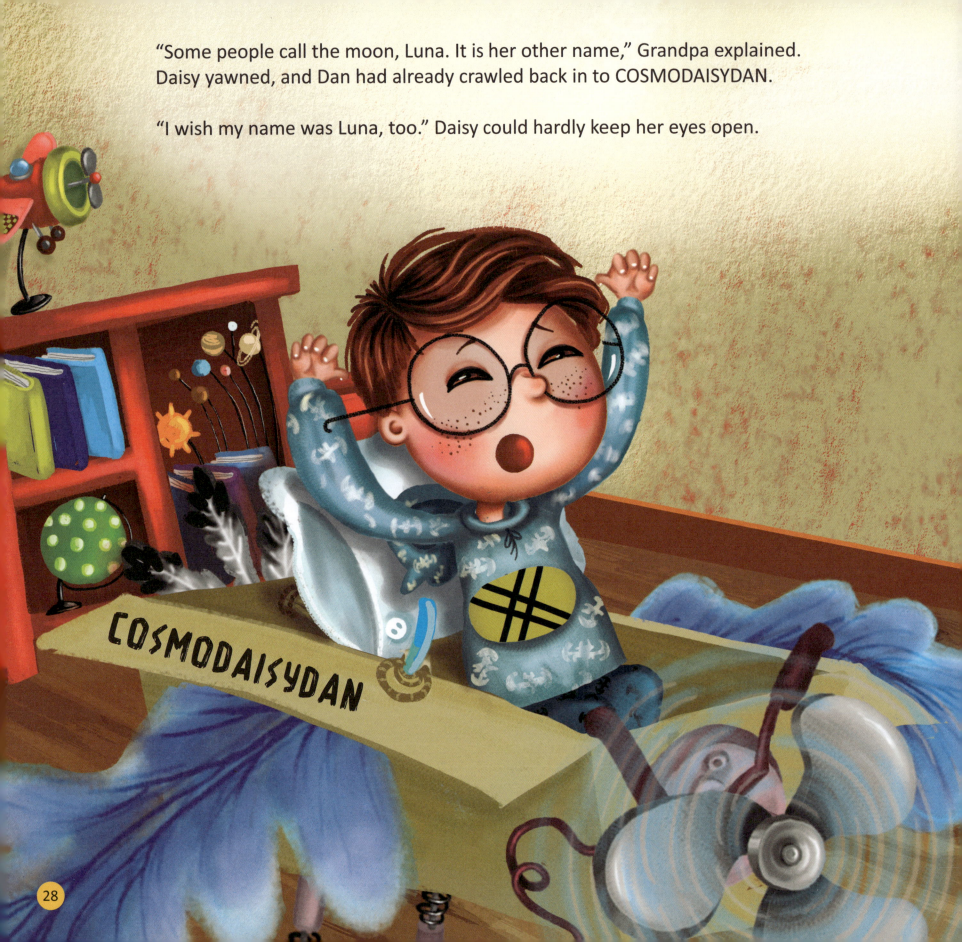

Grandpa smiled as she sat on his lap, "Daisy is a very lovely name."

"I think it's time for bed, little science explorers!"

Grandpa scooped Daisy up and placed her gently next to Dan.

"Night my little science explorers."

And off they went, exploring in their dreams ...

"In the infinite sky, there is a bright star, I love you Kay to the moon and back"

with love
Alexandra Colombo